The Cookie Recipe Book

for Sweet Lovers

50 Easy-to-Bake Cookie Recipes

BY: SOPHIA FREEMAN

HOME
FOOD
The best recipe

* * * * * * ★ ★ ★ * * * * *

* * * ★ ★ ★ ★ ★ ★ ★ * *

Table of Contents

Introduction

Cookies were the result of temperature checks in baking.

Since there weren't any thermostats invented yet, bakers would test small batches of the batter.

That's also why cookies were known as "little cakes."

There are as many as thousands of cookie varieties in the world.

For convenience, let's categorize them into eight types: drop, bar, molded, fried, refrigerator, sandwich, rolled, and no-bake cookies.

Drop cookies got their name since they are slowly dropped onto the baking sheet from 2 spoons. An excellent example of this is the chocolate chip cookie.

Bar cookies are what you get when you pour the batter into a pan and slice it into bars once baked, like the lemon cheesecake bar.

Molded cookie, such as Christmas cookies, are formed from the dough that is usually balled first, then pressed into molds to form different shapes and designs.

Fried cookies are just the deep-fried dough and are dusted with powdered sugar or drizzled with chocolate. An example is the deep-fried Oreo.

Refrigerator cookies are sometimes called icebox cookies since the dough needs to be chilled first before baking. An example would be the refrigerator sprinkle cookie.

Sandwich cookies are two cookies joined together with a sweet filling in between. A perfect example of this is the macaroon.

Rolled cookies are also referred to as cutouts since the dough needs to be rolled out flat with a rolling pin before cutting it into different shapes. Gingerbread men and cookies made with a cookie cutter are examples of this type.

No-bake cookies do not require any cooking at all. The cranberry chocolate marshmallow cookie is one tasty example of this type.

Many of the recipes you'll find here are drop cookies, but we'll cover the other types as well. Have fun!

Additional Interesting & Useful Information

- The first cookie could be traced back to Persia (now Iran) in the 7th century. It was only by the 14th century that the cookie became a hit in Europe.
- December 4th is celebrated as the National Cookie Day.
- August 4th is declared as the National Chocolate Chip Cookie Day and is dedicated to America's favorite cookie.
- The largest cookie ever made was by an American baking company in 2003. It was a gigantic chocolate chip cookie that measured 754 m^2 or 8,120 ft^2.
- The famous chocolate chip cookie was invented in the 1930s by Ruth Wakefield.
- Oreos remain the best-selling cookies in the US.

Chocolate Chip Cookies

Are you a fan of chunky chewy chocolate chip cookies? With this recipe, you can enjoy the classic chocolate chip cookies, which are indeed enough to send your sweet tooth to heaven.

Serving Size: 24

Preparation Cooking Time: 1 hour

Ingredients:

- 1 cup butter
- 1 cup brown sugar
- 1 cup white sugar
- 2 eggs
- 1 teaspoon baking soda mixed with 2 teaspoons hot water
- 2 teaspoons vanilla extract
- Salt to taste
- 3 cups all-purpose flour
- 1 cup walnuts, chopped
- 2 cups chocolate chips (semisweet)

Instructions:

1. Preheat your oven to 350 degrees F.

2. Soften the butter for a few minutes.

3. Transfer to a bowl.

4. Stir in the sugars and mix until fully combined.

5. Beat the eggs in another bowl.

6. Add to the butter mixture.

7. Add the vanilla extract and baking soda mixture.

8. Fold in the rest of the ingredients.

9. Form cookies from the mixture.

10. Place cookies on a baking pan.

11. Bake in the oven for 10 minutes.

Nutrients per Serving:

- Calories 298
- Fat 15.6 g
- Saturated Fat 8 g
- Carbohydrates 38.9 g
- Fiber 1.6 g
- Protein 3.6 g
- Cholesterol 36 mg
- Sugars 25 g
- Sodium 166 mg
- Potassium 110 mg

Sugar Cookies

Sweet and chewy sugar cookies that you can prepare plain or sprinkle with candies or nuts.

Serving Size: 48

Preparation Cooking Time: 30 minutes

Ingredients:

- ½ teaspoon baking powder
- 1 teaspoon baking soda
- 2 ¾ cups all-purpose flour
- 1 cup butter
- 1 ½ cups white sugar
- 1 teaspoon vanilla extract
- 1 egg, beaten

Instructions:

1. Preheat your oven to 375 degrees F.

2. Next, combine the flour, baking soda and baking powder in a bowl. Set aside.

3. Beat the butter and sugar in another bowl.

4. Stir in the vanilla and egg.

5. Gradually add the flour mixture to the butter mixture.

6. Next, form round shapes from the mixture.

7. Add these to a cookie pan.

8. Bake in the oven for 10 minutes.

9. Let cool on a wire rack.

Nutrients per Serving:

- Calories 85.9
- Fat 4 g
- Saturated Fat 2.5 g
- Carbohydrates 11.7 g
- Fiber 0.2 g
- Protein 0.9 g
- Cholesterol 14 mg
- Sugars 6.3 g
- Sodium 60.1 mg
- Potassium 10.5 mg

Coconut Cookies

Your sweet tooth's happy every time you bake these decadent coconut cookies, chewy on the outside and soft inside.

Serving Size: 36

Preparation Cooking Time: 50 minutes

Ingredients:

- 1 ¼ cups all-purpose flour
- ¼ teaspoon salt
- ½ teaspoon baking soda
- ½ cup butter
- ½ cup white sugar
- ½ cup brown sugar
- ½ teaspoon vanilla extract
- 1 egg, beaten
- 1 ½ cups coconut flakes

Instructions:

1. Preheat your oven to 350 degrees F.

2. Next, blend the flour, salt and baking soda in a bowl.

3. In another bowl, cream the sugars, butter, vanilla and egg.

4. Add the flour mixture to this bowl.

5. Then, drop a spoonful of the mixture on a baking pan.

6. Bake in the oven for 10 minutes.

Nutrients per Serving:

- Calories 75.4
- Fat 3.5 g
- Saturated Fat 2.4 g
- Carbohydrates 10.5 g
- Fiber 0.4 g
- Protein 0.7 g
- Cholesterol 11.9 mg
- Sugars 6.8 g
- Sodium 62.5 mg
- Potassium 21.4 mg

Ginger Cookies

Crystallized ginger makes these sweet crunchy cookies extra special. You're in for a big treat.

Serving Size: 18

Preparation Cooking Time: 30 minutes

Ingredients:

- 1 egg white
- ¾ cup butter
- 2 tablespoons corn syrup
- ½ cup white sugar
- 3 tablespoons crystallized ginger, chopped
- 1 teaspoon baking soda
- 2 cups all-purpose flour
- 1 teaspoon ground cloves
- 1 teaspoon ground ginger
- 1 ½ teaspoons ground cinnamon
- ¼ teaspoon salt
- ⅓ cup granulated sugar

Instructions:

1. Preheat your oven to 350 degrees F.

2. Brush baking sheets with the oil or butter.

3. In a bowl, beat the egg white, butter, corn syrup and sugar.

4. Add the chopped crystallized ginger.

5. In another bowl, combine the baking soda, flour, cloves, ground ginger, cinnamon and salt.

6. Add this mixture to the egg white mixture.

7. Knead the dough.

8. Form balls from the mixture.

9. Flatten each ball to form cookies.

10. Dip each cookie in granulated sugar.

11. Add to the baking sheet.

12. Bake in the oven for 15 minutes.

Nutrients per Serving:

- Calories 174.5
- Fat 7.8 g
- Saturated Fat 4.9 g
- Carbohydrates 24.9 g
- Fiber 0.5 g
- Protein 1.7 g
- Cholesterol 20.3 mg
- Sugars 12.4 g
- Sodium 111 mg
- Potassium 49.5 mg

Oatmeal Cookies

Oatmeal cookies are heavenly a dessert that you surely can't get enough of. These are loaded with fiber and other essential nutrients that are good for your health.

Serving Size: 24

Preparation Cooking Time: 2 hours

Ingredients:

- 2 eggs
- 2 cups all-purpose flour
- 1 cup brown sugar
- 1 cup white sugar
- 1 cup butter
- 1 teaspoon vanilla extract
- 1 teaspoon baking soda
- 3 cups oats (quick cooking)
- 1 ½ teaspoons ground cinnamon
- 1 teaspoon salt

Instructions:

1. Beat the eggs in a bowl.

2. Stir in the sugars, butter and vanilla extract.

3. Next, in another bowl, combine the dry ingredients: flour, baking soda, oats, ground cinnamon and salt.

4. Add this to the first bowl.

5. Mix well.

6. Cover the bowl.

7. Refrigerate for 1 hour.

8. Next, preheat your oven to 375 degrees F.

9. Brush your baking sheet with butter or oil.

10. Form cookies from the mixture.

11. Add cookies to the baking sheet.

12. Bake in the oven for 10 minutes.

Nutrients per Serving:

- Calories 218
- Fat 8.8 g
- Saturated Fat 5 g
- Carbohydrates 32.3 g
- Fiber 1.4 g
- Protein 3 g
- Cholesterol 36 mg
- Sugars 17 g
- Sodium 213 mg
- Potassium 69 mg

Peanut Butter Cookies

Did you know that the first peanut butter cookie was created in the United States in the 1910s? As the term implies, this type of cookie is made primarily with peanut butter.

Serving Size: 24

Preparation Cooking Time: 1 hour and 30 minutes

Ingredients:

- 1 cup butter
- 2 cups sugar
- 2 eggs
- 1 cup peanut butter
- ½ teaspoon salt
- 2 ½ cups all-purpose flour
- 1 ½ teaspoons baking soda
- 1 teaspoon baking powder

Instructions:

1. Preheat your oven to 375 degrees F.

2. Next, soften the butter and add to a bowl.

3. Stir in the sugar, eggs and peanut butter.

4. In another bowl, sift together the flour, baking soda, baking powder and salt.

5. Add the flour mixture to the butter mixture.

6. Mix well.

7. Next, cover the bowl.

8. Refrigerate for 1 hour.

9. Form round shapes from the mixture.

10. Place these on the baking pan.

11. Flatten the round shapes using a fork to create a pattern.

12. Bake in the oven for 10 minutes.

Nutrients per Serving:

- Calories 251.7
- Fat 13.6 g
- Saturated Fat 5.9 g
- Carbohydrates 29.7 g
- Fiber 1.2 g
- Protein 4.5 g
- Cholesterol 35.8 mg
- Sugars 18.2 g
- Sodium 209.4 mg
- Potassium 114.3 mg

Butter Cookies

Butter cookies are indeed a classic you can't go wrong with. These are very easy to make too.

Serving Size: 24

Preparation Cooking Time: 20 minutes

Ingredients:

- ½ cup butter
- 8 oz. cream cheese
- 18 oz. yellow cake mix
- ¼ teaspoon vanilla extract
- 1 egg, beaten
- ¼ cup confectioners' sugar

Instructions:

1. Preheat your oven to 350 degrees F.

2. Next, mix the butter and cream cheese in a bowl.

3. Stir in the cake mix, vanilla extra and egg.

4. Roll into balls.

5. Flatten the balls to form cookies.

6. Next, dust the cookies with the confectioners' sugar.

7. Arrange the cookies on the baking sheet.

8. Bake in the oven for 15 minutes.

Nutrients per Serving:

- Calories 167.5
- Fat 9.8 g
- Saturated Fat 4.9 g
- Carbohydrates 18.3 g
- Fiber 0.2 g
- Protein 2 g
- Cholesterol 28.6 mg
- Sugars 1.3 g
- Sodium 199.3 mg
- Potassium 32.8 mg

Pumpkin Cookies with Frosting

You can't stop eating these soft and chewy pumpkin cookies that only takes 10 minutes in the oven.

Serving Size: 18

Preparation Cooking Time: 30 minutes

Ingredients:

- 2 cups pumpkin puree
- 2 cups butter
- 2 eggs
- 2 cups white sugar
- 4 cups all-purpose flour
- 8 tablespoons milk
- 6 tablespoons butter
- 2 teaspoons baking soda
- 1 ½ teaspoons ground cinnamon
- 1 teaspoon salt
- 2 cups confectioners' sugar
- 1 cup brown sugar
- 1 ½ teaspoons vanilla extract

Instructions:

1. Preheat your oven to 350 degrees F.

2. In a bowl, mix the pumpkin, 2 cups butter, eggs and white sugar.

3. Sift in the flour, baking soda, salt and ground cinnamon.

4. Mix well.

5. Form cookies from the mixture.

6. Add the cookies to a baking sheet.

7. Bake in the oven for 10 minutes.

8. While waiting, make the frosting by heating the remaining ingredients in a pan over medium heat for 1 to 2 minutes.

9. Pour the frosting over the cookies and serve.

Nutrients per Serving:

- Calories 542.8
- Fat 27.7 g
- Saturated Fat 8.5 g
- Carbohydrates 71.4 g
- Fiber 1.6 g
- Protein 4.2 g
- Cholesterol 31.4 mg
- Sugars 48.5 g
- Sodium 376.6 mg
- Potassium 122.9 mg

Banana Cookies

Give yourself a treat with these potassium-packed cookies made with pureed banana, oats and dates.

Serving Size: 36

Preparation Cooking Time: 50 minutes

Ingredients:

- 3 ripe bananas
- ⅓ cup vegetable oil
- 1 teaspoon vanilla extract
- 1 cup dates, pitted and sliced
- 2 cups rolled oats

Instructions:

1. Preheat your oven to 350 degrees F.

2. Add the bananas to a food processor.

3. Next, pulse until pureed.

4. Transfer to a bowl.

5. Stir in the remaining ingredients.

6. Then, drop spoonfuls of the mixture on a baking pan.

7. Bake in the oven for 20 minutes.

Nutrients per Serving:

- Calories 56
- Fat 2.4 g
- Saturated Fat 0.2 g
- Carbohydrates 8.4 g
- Dietary Fiber 1 g
- Protein 0.8 g
- Cholesterol 0 mg
- Sugars 3.8 g
- Sodium 0.5 mg
- Potassium 78.5 mg

Jam Cookies

This sweet little treat is decadent and crunchy. When you get to the middle part, you'd love how the taste and texture of jam blends with the cookies.

Serving Size: 36

Preparation Cooking Time: 1 hour and 20 minutes

Ingredients:

- 2 egg yolks
- ½ cup white sugar
- ¾ cup butter, softened
- 1 ¾ cups all-purpose flour
- ½ cup fruit jam

Instructions:

1. Preheat your oven to 375 degrees F.

2. Next, in a bowl, mix the egg yolks, sugar and butter.

3. Stir in the flour.

4. Knead the dough.

5. Refrigerate for 1 hour.

6. Form balls from the mixture.

7. Add the balls to a baking sheet.

8. Next, flatten the balls to form cookies.

9. Press a hole in the center of the cookies.

10. Add a drop of jam to the center of the cookies.

11. Bake in the oven for 10 minutes.

Nutrients per Serving:

- Calories: 82
- Fat: 4.1g
- Saturated Fat: 2.5g
- Carbohydrates: 10.5g
- Fiber: 0.2g
- Protein: 0.8g
- Cholesterol: 21.5mg
- Sugars: 4.9g
- Sodium: 29.2mg
- Potassium: 12.1mg

Cream Cheese Sugar Cookies

In baking, cream cheese is typically added in the cake like in the popular blueberry cheesecake. But in this recipe, we use it to make heavenly sugar cookies.

Serving Size: 72

Preparation Cooking Time: 9 hours and 30 minutes

Ingredients:

- 3 oz. cream cheese
- 1 cup butter
- 1 egg yolk, beaten
- 1 cup white sugar
- 2 ¼ cups all-purpose flour
- ½ teaspoon almond extract
- ½ teaspoon salt
- ½ teaspoon vanilla extract

Instructions:

1. Beat the cream cheese, butter, egg yolk, sugar, vanilla extract, almond extract and salt in a bowl.

2. Mix well.

3. Gradually add the flour and stir.

4. Next, cover the dough and refrigerate for 8 hours.

5. Preheat your oven to 375 degrees F.

6. Roll out the dough on your kitchen table.

7. Use a rolling pin to spread it out.

8. Use a cookie cutter to create cookies from the dough.

9. Place the cookies on a baking sheet.

10. Lastly, bake in the oven for approximately 10 minutes or until golden.

Nutrients per Serving:

- Calories 52.6
- Fat 3.1g
- Saturated Fat 1.9g
- Carbohydrates 5.8g
- Fiber 0.1g
- Protein 0.6g
- Cholesterol 10.9mg
- Sugars 2.8g
- Sodium 38mg
- Potassium 6.7mg

White Chocolate Cookies with Macadamia

Truly, these white chocolate cookies dotted with macadamia nuts are a delightful treat. You only need 45 minutes to make a batch of more than 40 cookies.

Serving Size: 48

Preparation Cooking Time: 45 minutes

Ingredients:

- 2 ½ cups all-purpose flour
- 2 eggs
- 1 cup butter
- ½ teaspoon almond extract
- ¾ cup brown sugar
- ½ cup white sugar
- ½ teaspoon salt
- ½ teaspoon vanilla extract
- 1 teaspoon baking soda
- 1 cup macadamia nuts, chopped
- 1 cup white chocolate, chopped

Instructions:

1. Preheat your oven to 350 degrees F.

2. In a bowl, beat the eggs.

3. Stir in the sugars, butter, almond extract and vanilla extract.

4. Next, in another bowl, mix the flour, salt and baking soda.

5. Add the flour mixture to the egg mixture.

6. Fold in the white chocolate and macadamia nuts.

7. Then, drop spoonfuls of the mixture on a baking pan.

8. Bake in the oven for 10 minutes or until golden.

Nutrients per Serving:

- Calories 121.7
- Fat 7.4g
- Saturated Fat 3.6g
- Carbohydrates 13g
- Fiber 0.4g
- Protein 1.4g
- Cholesterol 18.7mg
- Sugars 7.7g
- Sodium 85.1mg
- Potassium 36.3mg

Molasses Cookies

Molasses refers to a sweetener made by processing beets or sugarcane. When used to make cookies, you get crustier and softer results.

Serving Size: 30

Preparation Cooking Time: 1 hour and 20 minutes

Ingredients:

- 2 cups all-purpose flour
- 1 ½ cups white sugar, divided
- ¾ cup margarine
- ¼ cup molasses
- 1 egg, beaten
- ½ teaspoon salt
- ½ teaspoon ground cloves
- ½ teaspoon ground ginger
- 1 teaspoon ground cinnamon
- 2 teaspoons baking soda
- ½ cup white sugar

Instructions:

1. First, melt the margarine in a pan over medium low heat, or in the microwave.

2. Add melted margarine to a bowl.

3. Stir in the egg, molasses and 1 cup white sugar.

4. In another bowl, mix the flour, baking soda, ginger, cloves, cinnamon and salt.

5. Gradually add this to the margarine mixture.

6. Next, cover the bowl.

7. Refrigerate for 1 hour.

8. Preheat your oven to 375 degrees F.

9. Form balls from the dough.

10. Roll each ball in the remaining sugar.

11. Flatten the balls to form cookies.

12. Add these to a baking sheet.

13. Bake for 10 minutes.

Nutrients per Serving:

- Calories 119.8
- Fat 4.7 g
- Saturated Fat 0.8 g
- Carbohydrates 18.6 g
- Fiber 0.3 g
- Protein 1.1 g
- Cholesterol 6.2 mg
- Sugars 11.6 g
- Sodium 178.8 mg
- Potassium 54.8 mg

Chocolate Mint Cookies

Expect these soft, chewy and decadent chocolate mint cookies to be gone seconds after you've put these on the table. It's a good thing; it only takes 30 minutes of active prep time to make as many as 3 dozen.

Serving Size: 18

Preparation Cooking Time: 1 hour and 30 minutes

Ingredients:

- ¾ cup butter
- 2 tablespoons water
- 1 ½ cups brown sugar
- 2 cups chocolate chips (semisweet)
- 2 eggs
- 2 ½ cups all-purpose flour
- 1 ¼ teaspoons baking soda
- ½ teaspoon salt
- Chocolate mint candies

Instructions:

1. First, in your saucepan over low heat, melt the butter and stir in the water and sugar.

2. Cook for 1 minute.

3. Stir in the chocolate chips.

4. Cook until melted.

5. Transfer mixture to a bowl and let cool.

6. Beat the eggs in a bowl, adding the flour, baking soda and salt.

7. Mix until fully combined.

8. Next, add this to the butter mixture and blend well.

9. Cover the bowl.

10. Refrigerate for 1 hour.

11. Preheat your oven to 350 degrees F.

12. Form balls from the dough.

13. Add the balls to a baking pan.

14. Flatten the balls to make cookies.

15. Bake in the oven for 10 minutes.

16. Lastly, take the cookies out of your oven and add mint candies on top.

Nutrients per Serving:

- Calories 364.3
- Fat 15.9 g
- Saturated Fat 9.7 g
- Carbohydrates 55.6 g
- Fiber 2 g
- Protein 3.7 g
- Cholesterol 41 mg
- Sugars 39 g
- Sodium 222 mg
- Potassium 148.4 mg

Peanut Butter Cookies with Kisses

You're undoubtedly going to have so much fun making these amazingly easy peanut butter cookies topped with your favorite chocolate kisses.

Serving Size: 9

Preparation Cooking Time: 1 hour and 20 minutes

Ingredients:

- 1 cup peanut butter
- 1 egg, beaten
- 1 cup white sugar
- 18 milk chocolate kisses

Instructions:

1. Preheat your oven to 350 degrees F.

2. Blend the peanut butter, egg and sugar in a bowl.

3. Combine sugar, peanut butter, and egg.

4. Next, cover the bowl and refrigerate for 1 hour.

5. Form balls from the mixture.

6. Flatten the balls and transfer to a cookie sheet.

7. Bake for 10 minutes.

8. Then, press a dent in the center of the cookie.

9. Top each one with a chocolate kiss.

Nutrients per Serving:

- Calories 311
- Fat 17.9 g
- Saturated Fat 4.9 g
- Carbohydrates 33.5 g
- Fiber 2 g
- Protein 8.5 g
- Cholesterol 22.7 mg
- Sugars 24.9 g
- Sodium 147.1 mg
- Potassium 230.3 mg

Chocolate Cookies with Caramel

Make your chocolate cookies extra special by filling them up with luscious caramel. It would surely feel like Christmas!

Serving Size: 24

Preparation Cooking Time: 2 hours and 30 minutes

Ingredients:

- 2 eggs, beaten
- 1 cup white sugar
- 1 cup butter
- 1 cup brown sugar
- 2 teaspoons vanilla extract
- 2 ¼ cups all-purpose flour
- ¾ cup cocoa powder (unsweetened)
- 1 teaspoon baking soda
- 1 cup walnuts, chopped and divided
- 1 tablespoon white sugar
- Caramel candies

Instructions:

1. Beat the butter until consistency is creamy.

2. Stir in the sugars, vanilla extract and eggs.

3. In another bowl, blend the flour, cocoa powder and baking soda.

4. Next, add the flour mixture to the first bowl. Mix well.

5. Add half of the walnuts.

6. Cover the bowl.

7. Refrigerate for 2 hours.

8. Preheat your oven to 375 degrees F.

9. Next, mix the remaining walnuts and remaining sugar. Set aside.

10. Form balls from the dough.

11. Press the caramel candies inside the balls.

12. Coat with the sugar and walnut mixture.

13. Flatten and add to a baking pan.

14. Then, bake in your oven for 8 to 10 minutes.

15. Let cool before removing cookies from the baking pan.

Nutrients per Serving:

- Calories 253
- Fat 13 g
- Saturated Fat 6.4 g
- Carbohydrates 33.1 g
- Fiber 1.6 g
- Protein 3.4 g
- Cholesterol 36.6 mg
- Sugars 21.9 g
- Sodium 127.5 mg
- Potassium 107 mg

Oatmeal Butterscotch Cookies

Do you love butterscotch bars? For sure, you're going to love these butterscotch cookies made with oats just as much!

Serving Size: 48

Preparation Cooking Time: 30 minutes

Ingredients:

- ¾ cup butter
- 2 eggs
- ¾ cup brown sugar
- ¾ cup white sugar
- ½ teaspoon salt
- 1 teaspoon baking soda
- 1 teaspoon vanilla extract
- 1 ¼ cups all-purpose flour
- 1 ⅔ cups butterscotch chips
- ½ teaspoon ground cinnamon
- 3 cups oats

Instructions:

1. Preheat your oven to 375 degrees F.

2. In a bowl, mix the eggs, sugars and vanilla extract.

3. In another bowl, combine the flour, ground cinnamon, baking soda and salt.

4. Add this to the first bowl.

5. Blend well.

6. Fold in the butterscotch chips and oats.

7. Drop spoonfuls of the mixture on a baking pan.

8. Bake in the oven for 10 minutes.

Nutrients per Serving:

- Calories 118.6
- Fat 5.1 g
- Saturated Fat 3.4 g
- Carbohydrates 16.2 g
- Fiber 0.6 g
- Protein 1.3 g
- Cholesterol 15.4 mg
- Sugars 10.3 g
- Sodium 81.4 mg
- Potassium 41.4 mg

Chocolate Chip Cookies with Banana

To make chocolate chip cookies even more delectably interesting, let's add mashed bananas into the mix. Bananas don't only add a creamy texture to the cookies but also make your cookies more nutritious.

Serving Size: 18

Preparation Cooking Time: 1 hour and 15 minutes

Ingredients:

- ¼ teaspoon baking soda
- 2 teaspoons baking powder
- 2 ½ cups all-purpose flour
- 2 eggs
- ½ teaspoon salt
- ⅔ cup butter, softened
- 1 cup white sugar
- 1 teaspoon vanilla extract
- 2 very ripe bananas, mashed
- 2 cups chocolate chips (semisweet)

Instructions:

1. Preheat your oven to 400 degrees F.

2. Brush your baking sheet with oil or butter.

3. In a bowl, sift together the flour, baking soda, baking powder and salt.

4. In another bowl, beat the eggs and stir in the butter, sugar and vanilla extract.

5. Add the mashed bananas to the second bowl.

6. Once fully combined, add the first bowl to the second bowl.

7. Mix well.

8. Form cookies from the mixture and arrange these on the baking sheet.

9. Bake in the oven for 15 minutes.

Nutrients per Serving:

- Calories 275.9
- Fat 13.2 g
- Saturated Fat 7.8 g
- Carbohydrates 39.2 g
- Fiber 1.9 g
- Protein 3.5 g
- Cholesterol 38.7 mg
- Sugars 22.9 g
- Sodium 195 mg
- Potassium 141.6 mg

Peanut Butter Cookies with Honey

Here's another fun way to make your peanut butter cookies—with honey, Greek yogurt and whole wheat flour!

Serving Size: 24

Preparation Cooking Time: 50 minutes

Ingredients:

- 1 teaspoon vanilla extract
- Cooking spray
- 1 cup whole wheat flour
- ⅔ cup peanut butter
- ¼ cup brown sugar
- ¼ cup Greek yogurt
- ½ cup honey
- 1 egg, beaten
- ½ teaspoon baking soda
- ⅛ teaspoon salt

Instructions:

1. Preheat your oven to 350 degrees F.

2. Spray your baking pan with oil.

3. Next, in a bowl, mix the honey, peanut butter and sugar.

4. Stir in the egg, vanilla extract and yogurt.

5. Use a mixer to mix until creamy.

6. Slowly add the flour, salt and baking soda.

7. Next, refrigerate for 30 minutes.

8. Form balls from the dough.

9. Flatten to make cookies using a fork to make a pattern.

10. Place the cookies on a baking pan.

11. Bake in the oven for 10 minutes.

Nutrients per Serving:

- Calories 96.1
- Fat 4.1 g
- Saturated Fat 0.6 g
- Carbohydrates 13.5 g
- Fiber 1.1 g
- Protein 3 g
- Cholesterol 7.8 mg
- Sugars 8.7 g
- Sodium 62.2 mg
- Potassium 79.6 mg

Triple Chocolate Cookies

These moist and chewy chocolate cookies are not just made with one or two chocolates but are made with three types of chocolates—dark, white and milk. This gives you the ultimate sweet treat.

Serving Size: 12

Preparation Cooking Time: 1 hour and 25 minutes

Ingredients:

- 1 egg
- ½ cup white sugar
- ¾ cup brown sugar
- ½ cup butter
- 1 teaspoon salt
- ¾ teaspoon baking soda
- 1 teaspoon vanilla extract
- 1 ½ cups all-purpose flour
- 1 cup milk chocolate chips
- 3 oz. dark chocolate chips
- 3 tablespoons white chocolate chips

Instructions:

1. Mix the sugars, butter and salt in a bowl.

2. Use an electric mixer to create creamy texture.

3. Stir in the vanilla and eggs.

4. Beat for 15 seconds.

5. In another bowl, combine the flour and baking soda.

6. Add this mixture to the sugar mixture.

7. Fold in the three chocolate chips.

8. Cover the bowl.

9. Refrigerate for 30 minutes.

10. Preheat your oven to 350 degrees F.

11. Form cookies from the mixture.

12. Place these in a baking pan.

13. Bake in the oven for 10 minutes.

14. Let cool for 30 minutes before serving.

Nutrients per Serving:

- Calories 193
- Fat 11.3 g
- Saturated Fat 5.0 g
- Carbohydrates 23.3 g
- Fiber 0.9 g
- Protein 2.1 g
- Cholesterol 20 mg
- Sugars 16 g
- Sodium 204 mg
- Potassium 36 mg

Chocolate Chip Oatmeal Cookies

This recipe combines your two favorites: chocolate chip cookies and oatmeal cookies. These have the chewy texture that you like, and the milky chocolate flavor you can't get enough of.

Serving Size: 42

Preparation Cooking Time: 1 hour

Ingredients:

- 2 eggs
- ½ cup white sugar
- 1 cup chocolate chips (semisweet)
- 1 cup brown sugar
- 1 cup butter
- ½ teaspoon baking soda
- 2 teaspoons vanilla extract
- 3 cups oats
- 1 ¼ cups all-purpose flour
- 1 cup walnuts, chopped
- 1 teaspoon salt

Instructions:

1. Preheat your oven to 325 degrees F.

2. In a bowl, beat the eggs.

3. Stir in the sugars, butter and vanilla extract.

4. Next, mix the baking soda, flour and salt in another bowl.

5. Add this to the egg mixture.

6. Add the oats, chocolate chips and walnuts.

7. Then, drop spoonfuls of the mixture on a cookie sheet to form the cookies.

8. Bake in the oven for 10 to 12 minutes.

Nutrients per Serving:

- Calories 144.7
- Fat 8.1 g
- Saturated Fat 3.8 g
- Carbohydrates 17.2 g
- Fiber 1.1 g
- Protein 2.1 g
- Cholesterol 20.5 mg
- Sugars 9.8 g
- Sodium 107.2 mg
- Potassium 63.6 mg

Oatmeal Raisin Cookies

Indulge yourself in these soft and chewy oatmeal cookies made more special with raisins.

Serving Size: 36

Preparation Cooking Time: 50 minutes

Ingredients:

- 1 cup butter
- 1 cup brown sugar
- ½ cup white sugar
- ½ teaspoon ground cloves
- 1 teaspoon vanilla extract
- 2 eggs, beaten
- ½ teaspoon salt
- 1 teaspoon baking soda
- 1 teaspoon ground cinnamon
- 1 ½ cups all-purpose flour
- 3 cups rolled oats
- 1 cup raisins

Instructions:

1. Preheat your oven to 350 degrees F.

2. Cream the butter, sugars, vanilla extract and eggs.

3. Mix until smooth.

4. In another bowl, mix the flour, cloves, cinnamon, salt and baking soda.

5. Add this to the first bowl.

6. Add the raisins and oats to the mixture.

7. Drop spoonfuls of the mixture onto the baking sheet.

8. Bake for 10 minutes.

9. Let cool before serving or storing.

Nutrients per Serving:

- Calories 144
- Fat 6.3g
- Saturated Fat 2.5g
- Carbohydrates 20.6g
- Fiber 1g
- Protein 1.9g
- Cholesterol 17.1mg
- Sugars 11.2g
- Sodium: 92.1mg
- Potassium: 73.6mg

Peanut Butter Cups

This buttermilk pie crust is an alternative to the traditional pastry crust. Additional ingredients like buttermilk and butter give this pie crust a delicious buttery flavor. To make this recipe extra.

Serving Size: 40

Preparation Cooking Time: 1 hour and 40 minutes

Ingredients:

- 1 ¾ cups all-purpose flour
- 40 chocolate peanut butter cups
- ½ cup butter
- ½ cup brown sugar
- ½ cup white sugar
- ½ cup peanut butter
- ½ teaspoon salt
- 1 teaspoon baking soda
- 2 tablespoons milk
- 1 teaspoon vanilla extract
- 1 egg, beaten

Instructions:

1. Preheat your oven to 375 degrees F.

2. Next, combine the baking soda, flour and salt in a bowl.

3. Cream the egg, butters, sugars, milk and vanilla extract.

4. Fold your flour mixture into the butter mixture.

5. Form balls from the dough and add these to a muffin pan.

6. Next, bake in the oven for 8 minutes.

7. Press the peanut butter cup into each of the balls.

8. Let cool before serving.

Nutrients per Serving:

- Calories 122
- Fat 6.5 g
- Saturated Fat 2.7 g
- Carbohydrates 14.4 g
- Fiber 0.6 g
- Protein 2.4 g
- Cholesterol 11.3 mg
- Sugars 9.2 g
- Sodium 119.1 mg
- Potassium 60.9 mg

Spiced Pumpkin Cookies

Here's the perfect afternoon treat for you and your family—spiced pumpkin cookies made with pumpkin puree, cinnamon, cloves and nutmeg.

Serving Size: 36

Preparation Cooking Time: 1 hour and 20 minutes

Ingredients:

- 1 teaspoon baking powder
- 1 teaspoon baking soda
- 2 ½ cups all-purpose flour
- ½ teaspoon salt
- ½ teaspoon ground cloves
- ½ teaspoon ground nutmeg
- 2 teaspoons ground cinnamon
- 1 egg, beaten
- ½ cup butter, softened
- 1 ½ cups white sugar
- 1 teaspoon vanilla extract
- 1 cup pumpkin puree
- 2 cups confectioners' sugar
- 1 tablespoon butter
- 1 teaspoon vanilla extract
- 3 tablespoons milk

Instructions:

1. Preheat your oven to 350 degrees F.

2. Next, mix the flour, cloves, nutmeg, cinnamon, baking soda, baking powder and salt in a bowl.

3. In another bowl, beat the eggs. Then, stir in the butter and sugar.

4. Add the vanilla extract and pumpkin puree.

5. Next, gradually add your flour mixture to the pumpkin mixture.

6. Drop the cookies by spoonfuls on the cookie baking sheet. Flatten with a spoon.

7. Bake in the oven for 20 minutes.

8. Let cookies cool.

9. In a pan over medium low heat, heat the remaining ingredients.

10. Drizzle the cookies with the glaze.

Nutrients per Serving:

- Calories 121.5
- Fat 3.2 g
- Saturated Fat 1.9 g
- Carbohydrates 22.4 g
- Fiber 0.5 g
- Protein 1.2 g
- Cholesterol 12.9 mg
- Sugars 15.2 g
- Sodium 120.5 mg
- Potassium 29.6 mg

Almond Cookies with Raspberry

For sure, you'll enjoy making these fancy-looking almond cookies with white glaze and raspberry jam.

Serving Size: 36

Preparation Cooking Time: 1 hour and 15 minutes

Ingredients:

- 2/3 cup white sugar
- 1 cup butter
- 2 cups all-purpose flour
- ¾ teaspoon almond extract
- ½ teaspoon almond extract
- 1 teaspoon milk
- ½ cup raspberry jam
- ½ cup confectioners' sugar

Instructions:

1. Preheat your oven to 350 degrees F.

2. Next, in a bowl, mix the sugar, butter and almond extract until smooth.

3. Add the flour and mix well.

4. Make several balls from the mixture.

5. Place the balls in the baking sheet.

6. Press a hole in the center.

7. Fill this hole with the raspberry jam.

8. Next, bake in the oven for 15 minutes.

9. Combine the remaining ingredients in another bowl.

10. Drizzle this mixture over the cookies.

Nutrients per Serving:

- Calories 103
- Fat 5.2 g
- Saturated Fat 3 g
- Carbohydrates 13.7 g
- Fiber 0.2 g
- Protein 0.8 g
- Cholesterol 14 mg
- Sugars 8 g
- Sodium 36 mg
- Potassium 9 mg

Chocolate Crinkles

These are not your usual drop cookies. These are a little softer and dredged with powdered sugar. It's like biting into a small piece of cake.

Serving Size: 72

Preparation Cooking Time: 5 hours

Ingredients:

- 1 cup cocoa powder (unsweetened)
- 2 cups all-purpose flour
- 2 cups white sugar
- ½ cup confectioners' sugar
- ½ cup vegetable oil
- 2 teaspoons vanilla extract
- 4 eggs, beaten
- 2 teaspoons baking powder
- ½ teaspoon salt

Instructions:

1. First, in a bowl, mix the vegetable oil, white sugar and cocoa powder.

2. Stir in the vanilla extract and eggs.

3. In another bowl, sift together the flour, salt and baking powder.

4. Cover the dough.

5. Refrigerate for 4 hours.

6. Preheat your oven to 350 degrees F.

7. Next, grease cookie sheet or line it with parchment paper.

8. Form balls from the dough.

9. Coat the balls with the confectioners' sugar and add to the cookie sheet.

10. Flatten the cookies.

11. Bake in the oven for 10 minutes.

Nutrients per Serving:

- Calories 58
- Fat 2 g
- Saturated Fat 0.0 g
- Carbohydrates 9.8 g
- Fiber 0.5 g
- Protein 0.9 g
- Cholesterol 10 mg
- Sugars 6 g
- Sodium 34 mg
- Potassium 26 mg

Pumpkin Choco Chip Cookies

This is a fusion of pumpkin pie and chocolate cookies—two sweet treats you enjoy having at home.

Serving Size: 24

Preparation Cooking Time: 30 minutes

Ingredients:

- ½ cup vegetable oil
- 1 cup white sugar
- 1 cup pumpkin puree
- 1 egg, beaten
- 2 cups all-purpose flour
- 1 tablespoon vanilla extract
- ½ teaspoon salt
- 2 teaspoons ground cinnamon
- 2 teaspoons baking powder
- 1 teaspoon milk
- 1 teaspoon baking soda
- ½ cup walnuts, chopped
- 2 cups chocolate chips (semisweet)

Instructions:

1. Mix the vegetable oil, white sugar, pumpkin puree and egg in a bowl.

2. Next, in another bowl, combine the flour, salt, cinnamon and baking powder.

3. Add the baking soda and milk to another bowl.

4. Add the baking soda mixture and flour mixture to the first bowl.

5. Next, fold in the rest of the ingredients.

6. Drop spoonfuls on a baking pan.

7. Bake in the oven at 350 degrees F for 10 minutes.

Nutrients per Serving:

- Calories 202.4
- Fat 10.7 g
- Saturated Fat 3.3 g
- Carbohydrates 26.6 g
- Fiber 1.7 g
- Protein 2.4 g
- Cholesterol 7.8 mg
- Sugars 16.5 g
- Sodium 170.9 mg
- Potassium 98.7 mg

White Chocolate Cookies with Cranberry

Creamy white chocolate cookies with chopped dried cranberries—these delicious cookies are most likely not to last long in the cookie jar. Before you know, all the cookies are gone!

Serving Size: 24

Preparation Cooking Time: 50 minutes

Ingredients:

- ½ cup butter
- ½ cup white sugar
- ½ cup brown sugar
- 1 egg, beaten
- 1 tablespoon brandy
- ½ teaspoon baking soda
- ¾ cup white chocolate chips
- 1 ½ cups all-purpose flour
- 1 cup dried cranberries, chopped

Instructions:

1. Preheat your oven to 375 degrees F.

2. Brush your baking sheet with oil.

3. Next, in a bowl, cream the sugars and butter.

4. Stir in the beaten eggs along with the brandy.

5. Sift together the baking soda and flour.

6. Add this to the butter mixture.

7. Next, fold in the cranberries and chocolate chips.

8. Drop spoonfuls of the mixture onto the baking pan.

9. Bake for 10 minutes.

Nutrients per Serving:

- Calories 147.4
- Fat 6.1 g
- Saturated Fat 3.7 g
- Carbohydrates 21.9 g
- Fiber 0.5 g
- Protein 1.5 g
- Cholesterol 19.1 mg
- Sugars 15.1 g
- Sodium 63.8 mg
- Potassium 18.5 mg

Orange Cookies with Cranberry

Orange and cranberry blend perfectly in this quick and easy cookie recipe that comes together in 35 minutes.

Serving Size: 48

Preparation Cooking Time: 35 minutes

Ingredients:

- 1 egg, beaten
- 1 cup butter
- ½ cup brown sugar
- 1 cup white sugar
- 1 teaspoon orange zest
- 2 tablespoons orange juice
- ½ teaspoon baking soda
- ½ teaspoon salt
- 2 ½ cups all-purpose flour
- ½ cup walnuts, chopped
- 2 cups cranberries, chopped
- 3 tablespoons orange juice
- ½ orange zest
- 1 ½ cups confectioners' sugar

Instructions:

1. Preheat your oven to 375 degrees F.

2. Mix the egg, butter and sugars in a bowl.

3. Stir in the orange juice and orange zest.

4. Blend the baking soda, salt and flour in another bowl.

5. Add this to the butter mixture.

6. Next, stir in the walnuts and cranberries.

7. Mix well.

8. Drop spoonfuls of the mixture onto baking sheet.

9. Bake in the oven for 15 minutes.

10. Let cool.

11. Mix the remaining ingredients.

12. Lastly, spread this mixture on top of the cookies.

Nutrients per Serving:

- Calories 110
- Fat 4.8 g
- Saturated Fat 3 g
- Carbohydrates 16.2 g
- Fiber 0.5 g
- Protein 1.1 g
- Cholesterol 14 mg
- Sugars 11 g
- Sodium 67 mg
- Potassium 25 mg

Gingersnap Cookies

Gingersnap cookies are healthy, thanks to ginger and cinnamon, which don't only add interesting flavors to crunchy cookies but are also loaded with antioxidants that are good for your body.

Serving Size: 30

Preparation Cooking Time: 30 minutes

Ingredients:

- ½ teaspoon salt
- 1 teaspoon ground cinnamon
- 2 teaspoons baking soda
- 2 cups all-purpose flour
- 1 tablespoon ground ginger
- 1 cup white sugar
- ¾ cup butter
- ¼ cup dark molasses
- 1 egg
- ⅓ cup cinnamon sugar

Instructions:

1. Preheat your oven to 350 degrees F.

2. Sift together the ginger, flour, cinnamon, baking soda and salt in a bowl.

3. Cream the sugar, butter, molasses and eggs in another bowl.

4. Next, add the flour mixture to the butter mixture.

5. Mix well.

6. Form balls from the mixture.

7. Roll the balls in the cinnamon sugar.

8. Next, place these in a baking sheet.

9. Flatten the balls to form cookies.

10. Bake in the oven for 10 minutes.

Nutrients per Serving:

- Calories 121.2
- Fat 5.4 g
- Saturated Fat 1.4 g
- Carbohydrates 17.5 g
- Fiber 0.3 g
- Protein 1.1 g
- Cholesterol 6.2 mg
- Sugars 8.2 g
- Sodium 126.3 mg
- Potassium 54.1 mg

Lemon Tea Cookies

You'll be delighted at how light, refreshing and filling these sugar cookies are. These are made with tea, lemon extract and corn syrup.

Serving Size: 48

Preparation Cooking Time: 2 hours

Ingredients:

- 1 egg
- ¾ cup butter
- 1 cup white sugar
- 1 teaspoon lemon extract
- 2 tablespoons corn syrup
- 2 cups all-purpose flour
- 1 teaspoon baking powder
- 1 teaspoon baking soda
- ½ cup white sugar

Instructions:

1. Beat the egg in a bowl.

2. Stir in the butter and white sugar.

3. Mix until fluffy.

4. Stir in the lemon extract and corn syrup.

5. Sift together the flour, baking powder and baking soda.

6. Add this to the butter mixture.

7. Cover the bowl.

8. Refrigerate for 1 hour.

9. Preheat your oven to 325 degrees F.

10. Roll the dough into smaller balls.

11. Roll the balls in the sugar and add to a baking pan.

12. Bake in the oven for 12 minutes.

Nutrients per Serving:

- Calories 72.6
- Fat 3 g
- Saturated Fat 1.9 g
- Carbohydrates 10.9 g
- Fiber 0.1 g
- Protein 0.7 g
- Cholesterol 11.5 mg
- Sugars 6.3 g
- Sodium 58.4 mg
- Potassium 8.1 mg

Brownie Cookies

Can't decide between brownies and cookies? Why not enjoy the best of these two heavenly treats? Make these brownie cookies, which will only take you a few minutes of active prep time.

Serving Size: 24

Preparation Cooking Time: 1 hour and 40 minutes

Ingredients:

- 1 cup all-purpose flour
- ¼ teaspoon baking soda
- ¼ cup butter
- ¼ cup brown sugar
- 2/3 cup granulated sugar
- 1/3 cup cocoa powder (unsweetened)
- 1 teaspoon vanilla extract
- ¼ cup buttermilk
- 1 tablespoon powdered sugar

Instructions:

1. First, sift the flour and baking soda into a bowl.

2. In a pan over medium heat, melt the butter.

3. Transfer the butter to another bowl.

4. Stir in the brown sugar, granulated sugar, cocoa powder, vanilla extract and buttermilk.

5. Next, add the flour mixture and mix well.

6. Cover the bowl.

7. Refrigerate for 1 hour.

8. Preheat your oven to 350 degrees F.

9. Grease your baking pan.

10. Next, drop spoonfuls of the mixture onto the baking pan.

11. Bake in the oven for 10 minutes.

12. Dust with the powdered sugar before serving.

Nutrients per Serving:

- Calories 246
- Fat 12.8 g
- Saturated Fat 8 g
- Carbohydrates 32.4 g
- Fiber 1.2 g
- Protein 2.8 g
- Cholesterol 52 mg
- Sugars 23 g
- Sodium 189 mg
- Potassium 99 mg

Apple Cookies

These apple cookies are not only eye candy but would definitely satisfy your cravings.

Serving Size: 18

Preparation Cooking Time: 1 hour and 30 minutes

Ingredients:

- ½ cup butter
- 1 1/3 cups brown sugar
- 1 egg
- 2 cups all-purpose flour
- ½ teaspoon salt
- ¼ teaspoon ground nutmeg
- ½ teaspoon ground cloves
- 1 teaspoon ground cinnamon
- 1 teaspoon baking soda
- 1 cup apples, diced
- 1 cup raisins
- 1 cup walnuts, chopped
- ¼ cup milk

Glaze

- 1 tablespoon butter
- 1 ½ cups confectioners' sugar
- 2 ½ tablespoons half-and-half cream
- ½ teaspoon vanilla extract

Instructions:

1. Cream the butter and sugar until fluffy.

2. Stir in the egg.

3. Next, in another bowl, mix the flour, salt, nutmeg, cloves, cinnamon and baking soda.

4. Add this to the butter mixture.

5. Fold in the apples, raisins and walnuts.

6. Pour in the milk.

7. Mix well.

8. Next, refrigerate for 1 hour.

9. Drop spoonfuls of this mixture onto baking pan.

10. Bake in the oven at 400 degrees F for 10 minutes.

11. Let cool.

12. Lastly, mix the glaze ingredients in a bowl and then spread on top of the cookies.

Nutrients per Serving:

- Calories 289
- Fat 11.4 g
- Saturated Fat 3 g
- Carbohydrates 45.7 g
- Fiber 1.4 g
- Protein 3.3 g
- Cholesterol 13 mg
- Sugars 32 g
- Sodium 151 mg
- Potassium 146 mg

Vegan Pumpkin Cookies

Thinking of turning into a vegan but doesn't want to give up your favorite sweet treats, right? Here's a vegan cookie recipe that you can make a home.

Serving Size: 18

Preparation Cooking Time: 1 hour

Ingredients:

- ¾ cup packed brown sugar
- ⅓ cup pumpkin puree
- ½ teaspoon salt
- 1 teaspoon baking soda
- 1 ½ teaspoons pumpkin pie spice
- 2 ¼ cups whole-wheat pastry flour
- ½ cup coconut oil
- 2 teaspoons vanilla extract
- 5 tablespoons maple syrup
- 1 cup vegan chocolate chips
- 1 ½ teaspoons sea salt

Instructions:

1. Preheat your oven to 375 degrees F.

2. Cover your baking pan with parchment paper.

3. In a bowl, mix the baking soda, salt, pumpkin pie spice and flour.

4. In another bowl, mix the coconut oil and brown sugar until smooth and creamy.

5. Next, stir in the vanilla extract, maple syrup and pumpkin puree.

6. Gradually add the flour mixture to the sugar mixture.

7. Drop spoonfuls of the mixture onto the baking pan.

8. Bake for 10 minutes.

9. Lastly, sprinkle the sea salt on top of the cookies.

Nutrients per Serving:

- Calories 223
- Fat 10.7 g
- Saturated fat 7.7 g
- Carbohydrates 31.2 g
- Fiber 2.5 g
- Protein 2.5 g
- Cholesterol 0 mg
- Sugars 18 g
- Sodium 329 mg
- Potassium 23 mg

Mexican Cookies

These traditional Mexican cookies are a wonderful treat for any occasion but are typically served during weddings. We make it a little different by replacing nuts with ground chocolate.

Serving Size: 40

Preparation Cooking Time: 20 minutes

Ingredients:

- 1 cup whole-wheat pastry flour
- 1 cup all-purpose flour
- ¼ cup granulated sugar
- ½ teaspoon salt
- 9 oz. dark chocolate, chopped
- 8 tablespoons butter, sliced into cubes
- 6 tablespoons grapeseed oil
- 2 teaspoons vanilla extract
- 1 tablespoon confectioners' sugar

Instructions:

1. Preheat your oven to 325 degrees F.

2. Add the flours, granulated sugar, salt and dark chocolate to a food processor.

3. Pulse until the chocolate is coarsely chopped.

4. Stir in the oil, butter and vanilla.

5. Pulse until clumpy.

6. Transfer to a bowl.

7. Form balls from the dough.

8. Add the balls to the baking pan.

9. Press the balls to flatten.

10. Bake in the oven for 20 minutes.

11. Dust the cookies with confectioners' sugar.

Nutrients per Serving:

- Calories 105
- Fat 7.2 g
- Saturated fat 3.2 g
- Carbohydrates 9 g
- Fiber 1.2 g
- Protein 1.3 g
- Cholesterol 6 mg
- Sugars 3 g
- Sodium 31 mg
- Potassium 61 mg

Fruit Oatmeal Cookies

Make your oatmeal cookies more special by adding currants, walnuts and dried apricots. These are not only sweet and delicious; these are also nutritious.

Serving Size: 48

Preparation Cooking Time: 40 minutes

Ingredients:

- 2 cups rolled oats
- Cooking spray
- ½ cup butter
- ¾ teaspoon baking soda
- 1 ½ cups brown sugar
- ¼ teaspoon ground allspice
- ¼ teaspoon salt
- 1 teaspoon vanilla extract
- 6 oz. yogurt
- 2 eggs, beaten
- 2 ¼ cups flour
- ¼ cup walnuts, chopped
- ¼ cup dried currants, chopped
- ¼ cup dried apricots, snipped

Instructions:

1. Preheat your oven to 375 degrees F.

2. Spread the rolled oats in a baking pan.

3. Bake in the oven for 10 minutes.

4. Spray your baking pan with oil. Set aside.

5. Use an electric mixer to beat the butter in a bowl.

6. Next, set it to medium speed and beat for 30 seconds.

7. Stir in the baking soda, brown sugar, allspices and salt.

8. Add the vanilla extract, yogurt and egg.

9. Gradually beat in the flour.

10. Fold in the remaining ingredients.

11. Mix well.

12. Then, drop spoonfuls of your mixture onto the baking pan.

13. Bake in the oven for 10 minutes.

Nutrients per Serving:

- Calories 101
- Fat 2.9 g
- Saturated fat 1.4 g
- Carbohydrates 16.9 g
- Fiber 1 g
- Protein 2.3 g
- Cholesterol 5 mg
- Sugars 8 g
- Sodium 55 mg
- Potassium 73 mg

Herb Butter Cookies

These fascinating cookies are actually easier to make than they look. You'll have fun pressing dried herb leaves onto the cookies to give each one a unique design.

Serving Size: 48

Preparation Cooking Time: 4 hours and 35 minutes

Ingredients:

- ½ cup butter
- 1 cup sugar
- 1 egg
- 1 ½ cups all-purpose flour
- ¼ teaspoon salt
- 1 teaspoon baking powder
- Fresh herbs and herb seeds (mint, thyme, tarragon, lavender, poppy, fennel)

Instructions:

1. Beat the butter using an electric mixer set to medium speed for 30 seconds.

2. Stir in the sugar and egg.

3. Gradually add the flour, salt and baking powder.

4. Mix well.

5. Divide the dough into 2.

6. Shape the dough into a log.

7. Cover and freeze for 4 hours.

8. Preheat your oven to 325 degrees F.

9. Cut the dough into rounds.

10. Press the herbs on top of the cookies.

11. Bake in the oven for 15 minutes.

Nutrients per Serving:

- Calories 48
- Fat 2 g
- Saturated fat 1 g
- Carbohydrates 7 g
- Fiber 2 g
- Protein 1 g
- Cholesterol 10 mg
- Sugars 2 g
- Sodium 33 mg
- Potassium 55 mg

Ice Cream Cookies

If you're fond of ice cream sandwiches, it'd certainly be a great idea to try the miniature version of these. Here's a recipe that lets you make these cute little ice cream cookies filled with vanilla cream.

Serving Size: 24

Preparation Cooking Time: 1 hour

Ingredients:

4 oz. cream cheese

- ½ cup butter
- 1 teaspoon cream of tartar
- ⅛ teaspoon salt
- 1 ¾ cups sugar
- 1 teaspoon baking soda
- ½ teaspoon vanilla bean paste
- 3 egg yolks
- ½ cup whole-wheat flour
- 1 ¼ cups all-purpose flour
- 3 cups vanilla ice cream

Instructions:

1. Preheat your oven to 300 degrees F.

2. Cream the butter and cream cheese for 30 seconds using a mixer set on medium speed.

3. Stir in the cream of tartar, salt, sugar and baking soda.

4. Mix until fully combined.

5. Stir in the vanilla bean paste and egg yolks.

6. Add the flours and mix.

7. Form balls from the dough.

8. Add the balls to a baking pan.

9. Bake in the oven for 15 minutes.

10. Spread one side of the cookies with the vanilla ice cream and put two cookies together to form a sandwich.

Nutrients per Serving:

- Calories 167
- Fat 6.3 g
- Saturated fat 3.7 g
- Carbohydrates 26.1 g
- Fiber 0.4 g
- Protein 2.3 g
- Cholesterol 39 mg
- Sugars 18 g
- Sodium 136 mg
- Potassium 42 mg

Walnut Raspberry Cookies

These colorful cookies give you incredible crunch and chewy texture with every bite. These are more than enough to brighten up your day!

Serving Size: 40

Preparation Cooking Time: 2 hours and 45 minutes

Ingredients:

- ¼ cup butter
- ¼ teaspoon ground cinnamon
- ¼ cup brown sugar
- ¼ cup granulated sugar
- ⅛ teaspoon baking soda
- ½ teaspoon baking powder
- ½ teaspoon vanilla
- 2 egg whites
- 1 cup rolled oats
- ¼ cup whole wheat flour
- ½ cup all-purpose flour
- 1 egg white, beaten
- ¾ cup walnuts, chopped
- ¼ cup raspberry jam

Instructions:

1. Beat the butter in a bowl using a mixer set to medium speed.

2. Mix for 30 seconds.

3. Add the ground cinnamon, sugars, baking soda and baking powder.

4. Beat until fully combined.

5. Stir in the vanilla and egg whites.

6. Fold in the oats and flours.

7. Cover the bowl.

8. Refrigerate for 2 hours.

9. Preheat your oven to 375 degrees F.

10. Line the baking pan with parchment paper.

11. Form balls from the mixture.

12. Roll the balls in the remaining egg white and dredge with the walnuts.

13. Press the balls in the center to create a dent.

14. Bake for 8 minutes.

15. Add the raspberry jam in the center of the cookies.

16. Let cool before serving.

Nutrients per Serving:

- Calories 61
- Fat 3 g
- Saturated fat 1 g
- Carbohydrates 7.5 g
- Fiber 0.5 g
- Protein 1.1 g
- Cholesterol 3 mg
- Sugars 4 g
- Sodium 23 mg
- Potassium 39 mg

Carrot Cake Cookies

Transform your favorite carrot cake into the cookies with this quick and easy-to-follow recipe.

Serving Size: 18

Preparation Cooking Time: 50 minutes

Ingredients:

- ½ cup honey
- ¼ cup brown sugar
- 1 tablespoon butter
- ¼ cup vegetable oil
- 1 egg
- 1 egg white
- 3 cups carrots, shredded
- ½ cup whole-wheat flour
- 2 cups all-purpose flour
- ½ teaspoon baking powder
- ½ teaspoon baking soda
- 1 ½ teaspoons pumpkin pie spice
- 1 cup walnuts, chopped
- 2 oz. low-fat cream cheese
- ½ cup powdered sugar

Instructions:

1. Preheat your oven to 350 degrees F.

2. Spray your baking pan with oil.

3. Mix the butter, honey and brown sugar using an electric mixer on medium speed.

4. Stir in the egg, egg white and oil.

5. Add the carrots and walnuts.

6. Drop spoonfuls onto baking pan.

7. Press to flatten.

8. Bake in the oven for 10 minutes.

9. Let cool on a wire rack.

10. Mix the remaining ingredients.

11. Drizzle the glaze over the cookies.

Nutrients per Serving:

- Calories 200
- Fat 8.1 g
- Saturated fat 1.5 g
- Carbohydrates 29.8 g
- Fiber 1.7 g
- Protein 3.7 g
- Cholesterol 16 mg
- Sugars 15 g
- Sodium 110 mg
- Potassium 131 mg

Tea Cookies

Yes, you can make your cookies using jasmine tea, and this is exactly what you'll learn from this recipe below.

Serving Size: 24

Preparation Cooking Time: 4 hours and 45 minutes

Ingredients:

- 1 teaspoon jasmine tea leaves
- ½ cup white whole wheat flour
- ½ cup cake flour
- 8 oz. cream cheese
- ¼ cup butter
- ⅛ teaspoon salt
- ½ cup granulated sugar
- ½ teaspoon vanilla extract
- 1 egg white
- Powdered sugar

Instructions:

1. Add the tea leaves and flours to a bowl. Set aside.

2. In another bowl, mix the cream cheese and butter using electric mixer set on high speed.

3. Mix for 30 seconds.

4. Stir in the salt and sugar.

5. Add the vanilla and egg white.

6. Mix for another 30 seconds.

7. Next, add the flour mixture. Then, mix until fully combined.

8. Cover the bowl.

9. Refrigerate for 4 hours.

10. Preheat your oven to 375 degrees F.

11. Form balls from the mixture.

12. Add the balls to a baking sheet.

13. Flatten the balls.

14. Next, bake for 10 minutes.

15. Let cool.

16. Dust with powdered sugar before serving.

Nutrients per Serving:

- Calories 59
- Fat 2.5 g
- Saturated fat 1.6 g
- Carbohydrates 8.4 g
- Fiber 0.3 g
- Protein 1 g
- Cholesterol 7 mg
- Sugars 4 g
- Sodium 38 mg
- Potassium 12 mg

Spiced Cookies

Make these paper-thin cookies if you're looking for a different kind of sweet treat.

Serving Size: 33

Preparation Cooking Time: 1 hour and 50 minutes

Ingredients:

- ½ teaspoon apple pie spice
- ½ teaspoon ground ginger
- ¼ teaspoon ground cardamom
- ¼ teaspoon ground cloves
- ⅛ teaspoon cayenne pepper
- 1 ⅓ cups all-purpose flour
- ⅓ cup butter
- ⅓ cup molasses
- ¼ cup brown sugar

Instructions:

1. Combine the apple pie spice, ginger, cardamom, cloves, cayenne pepper and flour in a bowl.

2. Next, in another bowl, cream the butter, sugar and molasses using an electric mixer set on medium speed.

3. Beat the mixture for 30 seconds.

4. Gradually beat in the flour mixture.

5. Mix until fully combined.

6. Cover the dough and refrigerate for 1 hour.

7. Divide the dough into 2.

8. Next, roll out each of the dough onto your kitchen table until the dough is only 1/16-inch thick.

9. Use a cookie cutter to form cookies from the dough.

10. Place the cookies on a baking sheet.

11. Bake in the oven at 375 degrees F for 5 minutes.

12. Let cool on a wire rack.

Nutrients per Serving:

- Calories 50
- Fat 2 g
- Saturated fat 1.2 g
- Carbohydrates 7.6 g
- Fiber 0.2 g
- Protein 0.5 g
- Cholesterol 5 mg
- Sugars 4 g
- Sodium 22 mg
- Potassium 60 mg

Plum Cookies

These plum cookies are moist, chewy and delicious. You'll have to stop yourself from eating the whole batch in one sitting!

Serving Size: 36

Preparation Cooking Time: 1 hour

Ingredients:

- Cooking spray
- 1 ¾ cups all-purpose flour
- 1 teaspoon baking soda
- 2 tablespoons brown sugar
- ¼ cup white sugar
- ⅛ teaspoon salt
- 1 oz. instant lemon pudding
- ⅓ cup canola oil
- 2 eggs
- 1 teaspoon almond extract
- 2.5 oz. pureed prunes
- ½ cup dried plums, pitted and chopped
- ½ cup almonds, toasted and sliced

Instructions:

1. Preheat your oven to 375 degrees F.

2. Spray your baking pan with oil.

3. Mix the flour, baking soda, sugars, salt and lemon pudding in a bowl.

4. Next, in another bowl, beat the eggs and stir in the almond extract and prunes.

5. Add this to the flour mixture.

6. Stir in the plums and almonds.

7. Drop spoonfuls of the mixture onto the baking pan.

8. Then, flatten using a fork.

9. Bake for 8 to 10 minutes.

Nutrients per Serving:

- Calories 70
- Fat 2.9 g
- Saturated fat 0.2 g
- Carbohydrates 10 g
- Fiber 0.6 g
- Protein 0.6 g
- Cholesterol 102 mg
- Sugars 3 g
- Sodium 86 mg
- Potassium 48 mg

Chocolate Cookies with Almonds Cherries

Among the various ways to make chocolate cookies, expect that this version with cherries and almonds is one that can easily become a favorite.

Serving Size: 24

Preparation Cooking Time: 2 hours

Ingredients:

- 6 tablespoons butter
- ¾ cup granulated sugar
- 1 teaspoon vanilla
- 1 egg yolk
- 1 egg
- 1 oz. semisweet chocolate, melted
- 1 ⅓ cups flour
- ½ cup dried cherries
- ⅓ cup almonds, sliced

Glaze

- ½ oz. semisweet chocolate, melted
- 1 ½ teaspoons butter
- ½ cup powdered sugar
- 1 tablespoon milk
- ¼ teaspoon almond extract

Instructions:

1. First, beat the butter in a bowl using an electric mixer set on medium high speed.

2. Mix for 2 minutes or until creamy.

3. Stir in the sugar, vanilla, egg yolk and egg.

4. Add the chocolate.

5. Mix for another 1 minute.

6. Fold in the flour, almonds and cherries.

7. Mix until fully combined.

8. Next, cover the bowl.

9. Refrigerate for 1 hour.

10. Preheat your oven to 350 degrees F.

11. Cover your baking sheet with parchment paper.

12. Form balls from the mixture.

13. Next, add the balls to the baking pan.

14. Flatten.

15. Bake for 10 minutes.

16. Let cool on a wire rack.

17. Mix the glaze ingredients in a over low heat.

18. Heat for 3 minutes, stirring frequently.

19. Let cool.

20. Drizzle the glaze on top of the cooled chocolate cookies.

21. Let sit until glaze has become firm.

Nutrients per Serving:

- Calories 88
- Fat 3.6 g
- Saturated fat 1.9 g
- Carbohydrates 13.5 g
- Fiber 0.4 g
- Protein 1.2 g
- Cholesterol 18 mg
- Sugars 9 g
- Sodium 25 mg
- Potassium 29 mg

Raisin Carrot Cookies

Yes, you can make raisin cookies using shredded carrots. For sure, you'll appreciate the chewy texture and delicious flavor of these cookies.

Serving Size: 36

Preparation Cooking Time: 50 minutes

Ingredients:

- ½ cup butter
- ¼ teaspoon salt
- 1 teaspoon ground ginger
- 1 teaspoon ground cinnamon
- 1 cup brown sugar
- 2 teaspoons baking soda
- 1 teaspoon vanilla extract
- 1 egg
- ¼ cup applesauce (unsweetened)
- 2 cups whole wheat flour
- ¾ cup walnuts, chopped
- ¾ cup raisins
- 2 carrots, shredded

Instructions:

1. Preheat your oven to 375 degrees F.

2. Beat the butter in a bowl for 30 second using an electric mixer set on medium speed.

3. Stir in the salt, ginger, cinnamon, sugar and baking soda.

4. Next, add the vanilla extract, egg and applesauce.

5. Add the flour and the rest of the ingredients to the mixture.

6. Mix until fully combined.

7. Next, drop spoonfuls of the mixture onto a baking sheet.

8. Bake in the oven for 8 to 10 minutes.

9. Let cool on a wire rack.

Nutrients per Serving:

- Calories 98
- Fat 4 g
- Saturated fat 2 g
- Carbohydrates 14 g
- Fiber 1 g
- Protein 2 g
- Cholesterol 12 mg
- Sugars 8 g
- Sodium 115 mg
- Potassium 335 mg

Almond Crescent Cookies

Enjoy these crescent cookies made with almonds and drizzled with chocolate sauce after a meal or as a snack in the afternoon.

Serving Size: 32

Preparation Cooking Time: 45 minutes

Ingredients:

- Cooking spray
- 2 ¼ cups almonds
- ¾ cup sugar
- 1 teaspoon almond extract
- 2 egg whites
- 2 tablespoons almond slices
- Melted chocolate

Instructions:

1. Preheat your oven to 350 degrees F.

2. Cover your baking pan with parchment paper.

3. Add the whole almonds and sugar to a food processor.

4. Pulse until powdery.

5. Add the almond extract and egg whites.

6. Process until smooth.

7. Add spoonfuls of the mixture on a baking pan.

8. Shape these into a crescent.

9. Add the almond slices on top of the cookies.

10. Bake in the oven for 10 minutes.

11. Let cool.

12. Drizzle with the melted chocolate.

Nutrients per Serving:

- Calories 80
- Fat 5.3 g
- Saturated fat 0.4 g
- Carbohydrates 6.7 g
- Fiber 1.2 g
- Protein 2.4 g
- Cholesterol 102 mg
- Sugars 5 g
- Sodium 4 mg
- Potassium 79 mg

Vegan Crunchy Cookies

Here's another vegan cookie recipe that you'll surely enjoy making. What makes this different from the previous one, though, is that this doesn't require baking in the oven.

Serving Size: 22

Preparation Cooking Time: 2 hours and 20 minutes

Ingredients:

- ¾ cup almond butter
- ¼ cup coconut oil
- ¼ cup almond milk (unsweetened)
- ⅓ cup brown sugar
- 1 teaspoon vanilla extract
- 1 teaspoon ground cinnamon
- 1 ¾ cups rolled oats
- ⅛ teaspoon salt

Instructions:

1. First, in a pan over medium heat, add the almond butter, coconut oil, almond milk and brown sugar.

2. Cook while stirring until the sugar has been dissolved.

3. Stir in the rest of the ingredients.

4. Next, cook for 2 minutes, stirring frequently.

5. Turn off the heat and let cool.

6. Then, drop spoonfuls of your mixture onto a baking pan.

7. Refrigerate for 2 hours.

Nutrients per Serving:

- Calories 113
- Fat 7.8 g
- Saturated fat 2.7 g
- Carbohydrates 9.3 g
- Fiber 1.6 g
- Protein 2.6 g
- Cholesterol 92 mg
- Sugars 4 g
- Sodium 36 mg
- Potassium 95 mg

Cherry Cookies

These cherry cookies are as chunky as you'd want your cookies to be. These are made with chocolate, cherries, and rolled oats.

Serving Size: 28

Preparation Cooking Time: 50 minutes

Ingredients:

- ⅛ teaspoon salt
- ½ cup dried cherries, chopped
- 1/3 cup brown sugar
- ¼ cup vegetable oil spread
- ½ teaspoon baking soda
- 1 teaspoon vanilla extract
- 2 tablespoons cocoa powder
- 1 egg
- ⅔ cup all-purpose flour
- ¼ cup flax seed meal
- ⅔ cup rolled oats
- 4 oz. dark chocolate, chopped
- 2 oz. white baking chocolate, chopped

Instructions:

1. Preheat your oven to 350 degrees F.

2. Cover your baking pan with parchment paper.

3. In a bowl, mix the vegetable oil, baking soda, salt and brown sugar.

4. Use an electric mixer set on medium speed to beat the mixture for 30 seconds.

5. Stir in the cocoa powder, vanilla extract and egg.

6. Next, mix for 10 to 20 seconds.

7. Fold in the flour, flax seed meal and oats.

8. Add the rest of the ingredients.

9. Mix until fully combined.

10. Then, drop spoonfuls of this mixture on the baking pan.

11. Bake in the oven for 10 minutes.

Nutrients per Serving:

- Calories 84
- Fat 4.1 g
- Saturated fat 1.8 g
- Carbohydrates 14.2 g
- Fiber 1 g
- Protein 1.5 g
- Cholesterol 72 mg
- Sugars 9 g
- Sodium 53 mg
- Potassium 58 mg

Lemon Cookies

These cheerful lemon cookies that resemble sunshine are definitely more than enough to brighten up your day.

Serving Size: 48

Preparation Cooking Time: 2 hours and 10 minutes

Ingredients:

Lemon Curd

- ½ cup granulated sugar
- ¾ cup butter
- ¼ cup lemon juice
- 2 teaspoons lemon zest
- 1 egg yolk

Cookies

- ¼ cup butter
- ⅔ cup granulated sugar
- 4 teaspoons lemon zest
- 2 egg whites
- 1 tablespoon vanilla
- 2 tablespoons lemon juice
- 1 tablespoon lemon zest
- 2 ¼ cups all-purpose flour
- ¼ cup cornstarch
- ½ teaspoon baking powder
- ½ teaspoon salt

Instructions:

1. First, to make the lemon curd, add the sugar and butter to a bowl.

2. Mix well.

3. Stir in the lemon juice, lemon zest and egg yolk.

4. Add this mixture to a pan over low heat.

5. Cook while stirring for 3 minutes or until the mixture has slightly thickened.

6. Transfer the mixture to a bowl.

7. Let cool.

8. Cover and refrigerate for 1 hour.

9. Next, prepare the cookies.

10. Preheat your oven to 350 degrees F.

11. Cover your baking pan with parchment paper.

12. In a bowl, mix the remaining butter and granulated sugar.

13. Stir in the lemon zest, egg whites and vanilla extract.

14. Add the lemon juice.

15. In another bowl, combine the remaining ingredients.

16. Add this mixture to the butter mixture.

17. Next, mix to form dough.

18. Refrigerate dough for 1 hour.

19. Form balls from the dough.

20. Add the balls to a baking pan.

21. Flatten the balls to form cookies.

22. Gradually make an indentation in the middle of the cookies.

23. Bake in the oven for 15 minutes.

24. Let cool on the wire rack.

25. Add the lemon curd in the center of the cookies.

Nutrients per Serving:

- Calories 73
- Fat 3 g
- Saturated fat 1.9 g
- Carbohydrates 10.6 g
- Fiber 0.2 g
- Protein 0.9 g
- Cholesterol 11 mg
- Sugars 5 g
- Sodium 55 mg
- Potassium 13 mg

Chocolate Zucchini Cookies

You probably wouldn't have imagined that you can actually use zucchini to make decadent chocolate cookies. This cookie recipe is a wonderful surprise.

Serving Size: 30

Preparation Cooking Time: 1 hour

Ingredients:

- 1 cup butter
- 1 cup brown sugar
- 1 teaspoon vanilla extract
- 2 eggs
- 8 oz. dark chocolate, chopped
- 1 ½ cups rolled oats
- 1 ½ cups whole-wheat flour
- 1 zucchini, shredded and dried
- ½ teaspoon salt
- ½ teaspoon ground cinnamon
- ½ teaspoon baking soda
- 1 teaspoon baking powder
- ¼ teaspoon ground nutmeg

Instructions:

1. Combine the butter, vanilla extract and brown sugar in a bowl.

2. Use an electric mixer set to medium speed to beat this mixture for 1 minute.

3. Add the eggs and beat for 10 seconds.

4. In another bowl, combine the oats, nutmeg, baking powder, baking soda, flour, cinnamon and salt.

5. Add this to the butter mixture.

6. Stir in the chocolate and zucchini.

7. Beat on low to medium speed until fully combined.

8. Cover the dough and refrigerate for 30 minutes.

9. Preheat your oven to 350 degrees F.

10. Cover your baking pan with parchment paper.

11. Drop spoonfuls of the mixture to the baking pan.

12. Bake for 15 minutes.

Nutrients per Serving:

- Calories 173
- Fat 10.2 g
- Saturated fat 5.9 g
- Carbohydrates 18.7 g
- Fiber 2 g
- Protein 2.6 g
- Cholesterol 29 mg
- Sugars 9 g
- Sodium 163 mg
- Potassium 125 mg

Conclusion

The delightful taste and smell of freshly baked cookies are really hard to resist.

Making and designing cookies is a fun and wonderful way to bond with your family and friends.

They are great to snack on and go well with our favorite beverages, like milk, coffee, and tea.

Cookies are small enough to carry anywhere, which also makes them the ideal pick-me-up.

Whether you like your cookies soft and chewy or crispy and crumbly, there is always a cookie that will suit your liking and instantly lift your mood.

About the Author

A native of Albuquerque, New Mexico, Sophia Freeman found her calling in the culinary arts when she enrolled at the Sante Fe School of Cooking. Freeman decided to take a year after graduation and travel around Europe, sampling the cuisine from small bistros and family owned restaurants from Italy to Portugal. Her bubbly personality and inquisitive nature made her popular with the locals in the villages and when she finished her trip and came home, she had made friends for life in the places she had visited. She also came home with a deeper understanding of European cuisine.

Freeman went to work at one of Albuquerque's 5-star restaurants as a sous-chef and soon worked her way up to head chef. The restaurant began to feature Freeman's original dishes as specials on the menu and soon after, she began to write e-books with her recipes. Sophia's dishes mix local flavours with European inspiration making them irresistible to the diners in her restaurant and the online community.

Freeman's experience in Europe didn't just teach her new ways of cooking, but also unique methods of presentation. Using rich sauces, crisp vegetables and meat cooked to perfection, she creates a stunning display as well as a delectable dish. She has won many local awards for her cuisine and she continues to delight her diners with her culinary masterpieces.

* * * * ★ ★ ★ ★ ★ * * *

Author's Afterthoughts

I want to convey my big thanks to all of my readers who have taken the time to read my book. Readers like you make my work so rewarding and I cherish each and every one of you.

Grateful cannot describe how I feel when I know that someone has chosen my work over all of the choices available online. I hope you enjoyed the book as much as I enjoyed writing it.

Feedback from my readers is how I grow and learn as a chef and an author. Please take the time to let me know your thoughts by leaving a review on Amazon so I and your fellow readers can learn from your experience.

My deepest thanks,

Sophia Freeman

Subscribe to the Newsletter!

Your email address   Subscribe

https://sophia.subscribemenow.com/

* * * * ★ ★ ★ ★ ★ * * *

Made in the USA
Monee, IL
05 May 2022

95903673R00092